INDONESIA

Robin Lim

Lerner Publications Company • Minneapolis

Lerner Publications Company
A division of Lerner Publishing Group, Inc.
241 First Avenue North
Minneapolis, MN 55401 U.S.A.

Website address: www.lernerbooks.com

Library of Congress Cataloging-in-Publication Data

Lim, Robin, 1956–
    Indonesia / by Robin Lim.
      p. cm. — (Country explorers)
    Includes bibliographical references and index.
    ISBN 978–1–58013–602–0 (lib. bdg. : alk. paper)
     1. Indonesia—Juvenile literature. I. Title.
DS615.L55 2010
959.8—dc22   2009019478

Manufactured in the United States of America
1 – VI – 12/15/09

Table of Contents

Welcome!

Let's explore Indonesia. This country is made up of more than thirteen thousand islands. The islands lie in the waters between the continents of Australia and Asia. Two oceans and ten seas touch the islands. The Pacific Ocean is northeast of Indonesia. The Indian Ocean is to the southwest. In the southeast lie the Arafura and Timor seas. Those seas separate Indonesia from Australia. And to the north, the Celebes Sea and the Sulu Sea separate Indonesia from the Philippines.

SOUTH CHINA SEA

ASAHAN RIVER

HARI RIVER

MUSI RIVER

JAVA

ANAK KRAKATAU

Jakarta

Komodo Island lies in southern Indonesia between the Bali Sea and the Timor Sea.

Lots of Islands

Indonesia's biggest islands are Borneo, Sumatra, Irian Jaya, Java, Flores, Bali, Sulawesi (Celebes), and West Timor. Most of the people of Indonesia live on the island of Java. Jakarta, the nation's capital, is on Java.

Fireworks sparkle over the city of Jakarta.

6

A big plain covers the middle of Bali. Volcanoes rise up in the north. Tiny Flores has fourteen volcanoes. Sumatra is dotted with forests, rain forests, swamps, and mountains.

Thick forests cover much of the island of Sumatra.

Earthquake!

The islands of Indonesia have a lot of earthquakes. During an earthquake, parts of the earth shift. This shift makes the ground move. Some earthquakes cause great damage. In 2004, an earthquake near Sumatra made the ocean floor move. The earthquake created a huge tsunami, or tidal wave. The tsunami hit Sumatra and other islands.

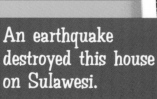

An earthquake destroyed this house on Sulawesi.

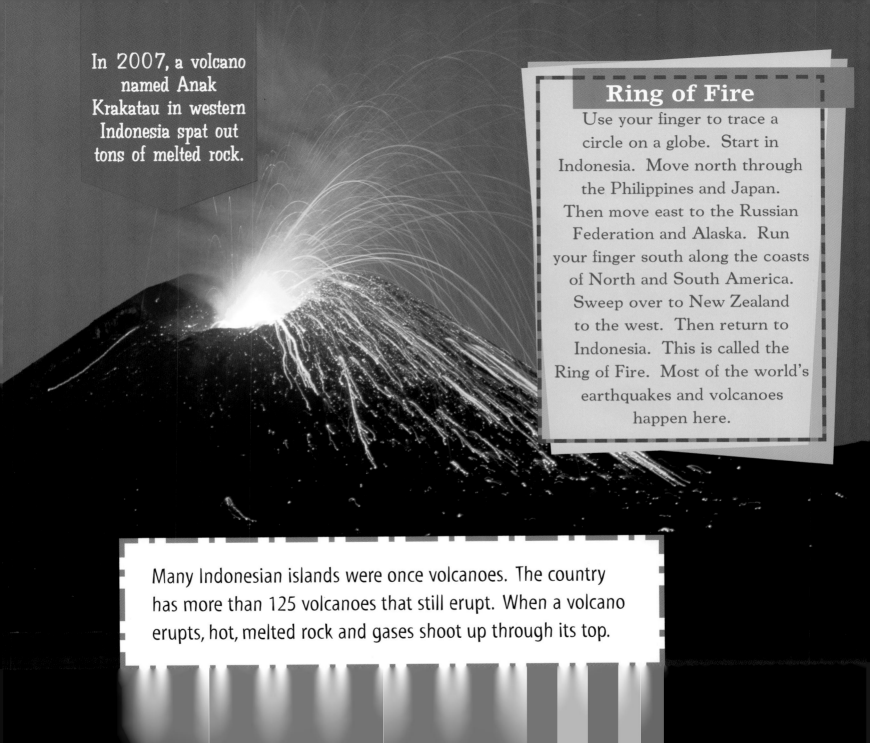

In 2007, a volcano named Anak Krakatau in western Indonesia spat out tons of melted rock.

Ring of Fire

Use your finger to trace a circle on a globe. Start in Indonesia. Move north through the Philippines and Japan. Then move east to the Russian Federation and Alaska. Run your finger south along the coasts of North and South America. Sweep over to New Zealand to the west. Then return to Indonesia. This is called the Ring of Fire. Most of the world's earthquakes and volcanoes happen here.

Many Indonesian islands were once volcanoes. The country has more than 125 volcanoes that still erupt. When a volcano erupts, hot, melted rock and gases shoot up through its top.

Big Wildlife

Thousands of plants cover the Indonesian islands. The *rafflesia arnoldii* is the biggest flower in the world. It grows in the rain forests of Sumatra. Sumatra is also home to lots of animals. Rhinoceroses, orangutans, Sumatran tigers, tapirs, and elephants live there.

The flower of the *rafflesia arnoldii* looks pretty, but it smells terrible!

Indonesia's Queen Alexandra's Birdwing is the world's largest butterfly. Its wings stretch 11 inches (28 centimeters) from the tip of one wing to the tip of the other. That is as long as your arm!

Dear Grandpa,
Yesterday we took a ferry to the island of Komodo to see the dragons. Wow! Komodo dragons have scales like fish. They can grow to be more than 12 feet (4 meters) long. The dragons use their tongues to smell. Komodo dragons have more than sixty teeth. And boy, are they sharp! I wanted to take a dragon home, but Mom said, "No way."

See you soon!

Chris

Komodo dragon • Komodo Island

Your Fr
Your T
Anywhe

First People

The Malay people arrived in Indonesia four thousand years ago. They came from Southeast Asia. Before then, no people had lived in Indonesia. The Malay built wooden houses on the coasts. They wove cloth. And they made pottery bowls. They grew rice to eat.

Malay houses sit on stilts. This keeps the houses dry during the rainy season from November to April.

12

More Malay people arrived in Indonesia almost two thousand years later. This group ate rice and other plants.

Java Man

More than one hundred years ago, scientists dug up a skull *(below)* in central Java. They called it Java Man. He was an early relative of humans. Java Man lived five hundred thousand years ago. Since then, scientists have found more bones in Indonesia. They are even older than Java Man.

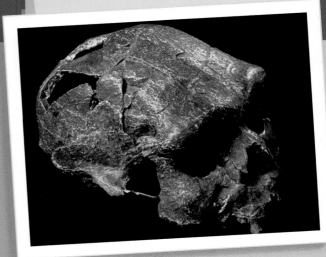

Malay people in Indonesia still grow rice on their farms.

Many Peoples

Indonesia has about three hundred different ethnic groups. They include the Javanese, the Sundanese, the Madurese, the Kubu, the Malay, and the Batak. Many of Indonesia's political leaders are Javanese. The Sundanese mainly farm rice fields in western Java. Many Madurese live in eastern Java. The Madurese are from Madura, an island northeast of Java.

These Madurese women live on the island of Madura.

14

On Sumatra, the Kubu live along the eastern coast. The Batak grow rice in the valleys of northern Sumatra.

Most of the Kubu people live in Sumatra's forests.

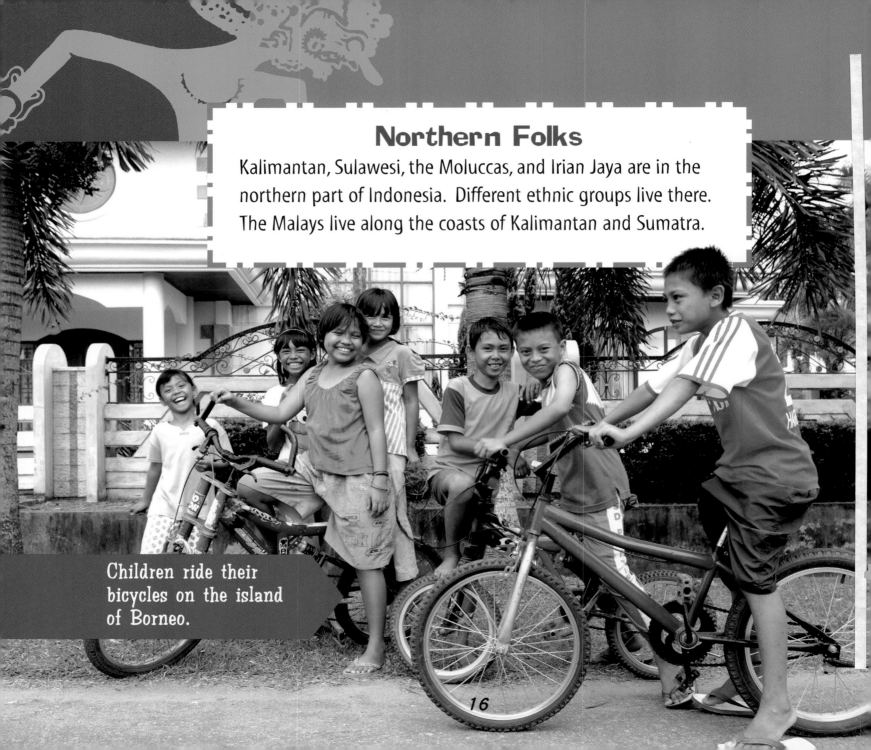

Northern Folks

Kalimantan, Sulawesi, the Moluccas, and Irian Jaya are in the northern part of Indonesia. Different ethnic groups live there. The Malays live along the coasts of Kalimantan and Sumatra.

Children ride their bicycles on the island of Borneo.

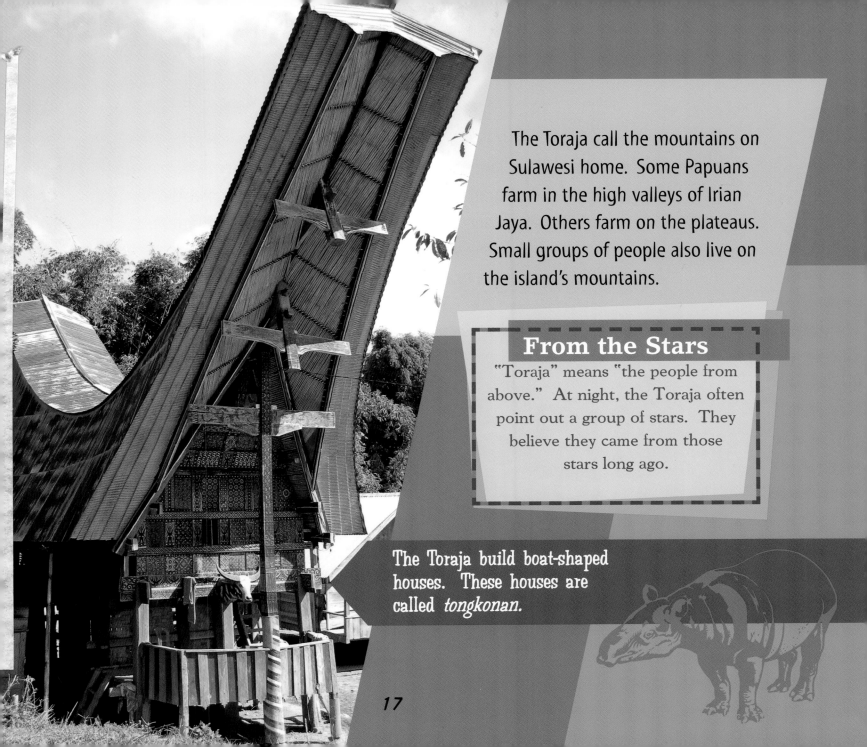

The Toraja call the mountains on Sulawesi home. Some Papuans farm in the high valleys of Irian Jaya. Others farm on the plateaus. Small groups of people also live on the island's mountains.

From the Stars

"Toraja" means "the people from above." At night, the Toraja often point out a group of stars. They believe they came from those stars long ago.

The Toraja build boat-shaped houses. These houses are called *tongkonan*.

17

Family

In Indonesian villages, lots of kids live with their parents, brothers, sisters, grandparents, aunts, uncles, and cousins. All the adults take turns caring for the kids. Family life is different in the cities. Kids live with just their parents, brothers, and sisters. Sometimes a grandparent lives there too.

This family lives on one of Indonesia's northern islands.

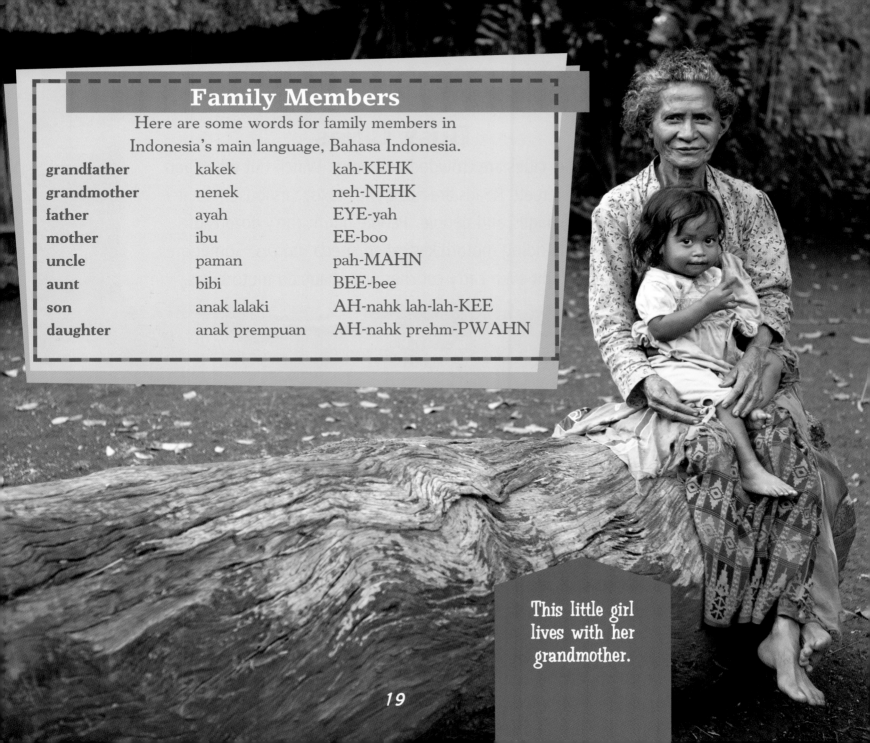

Family Members

Here are some words for family members in Indonesia's main language, Bahasa Indonesia.

grandfather	kakek	kah-KEHK
grandmother	nenek	neh-NEHK
father	ayah	EYE-yah
mother	ibu	EE-boo
uncle	paman	pah-MAHN
aunt	bibi	BEE-bee
son	anak lalaki	AH-nahk lah-lah-KEE
daughter	anak prempuan	AH-nahk prehm-PWAHN

This little girl lives with her grandmother.

Busy Cities

Indonesia's cities are crowded and noisy. Watch out when you cross the street! Roads are filled with taxis, cars, buses, horse-drawn carriages, and people. People might carry dozens of eggs while riding motorbikes called *speda motors*. Sometimes, people might even carry couches and chairs on motorbikes.

Cars and motorbikes drive on sidewalks during rush hour in Jakarta.

In Jakarta, new office buildings, department stores, and hotels reach to the sky. Most families live in concrete houses. The houses have tile roofs. Many poor people live in tiny wood and cardboard houses. These houses have tin roofs.

These children live in a colorful concrete house.

A family ties bundles of grass onto the roof of their home on Flores Island.

Country Living

What kinds of chores do you have at home? In the country, Indonesian kids help make grass roofs for their homes. These kids also feed the pigs. They even pluck feathers from freshly killed chickens. Later, the chickens will be cooked for dinner.

On Indonesian farms, kids protect the growing rice from hungry birds. They run through the rice fields. They yell and wave their arms. That scares away the birds. Putting scarecrows in the fields also helps. To birds, scarecrows look like people.

Farmers wave flags and noisemakers to keep birds out of the rice fields. Scarecrows help too.

23

Speak Up!

In Indonesia, people use more than 365 languages. Most Indonesians speak at least two languages. At home, kids speak the language their parents use. At school, kids learn Bahasa Indonesia. That means "language of Indonesia." It's the nation's official language. Bahasa is based on the Malay and Javanese languages. When kids get older, some learn English.

24

A boy reads at a school in Jakarta.

Greet an Indonesian

Here are a few greetings in Bahasa Indonesia. Try them out on a friend!

blessings on your morning	selamat pagi	shee-lah-MAHT PAH-gee
blessings on your midday	selamat siang	shee-lah-MAHT see-AHNG
blessings on your late day	selamat sore	shee-lah-MAHT soh-RAY
blessings on your night	selamat malam	shee-lah-MAHT mah-LAHM
blessings on your sleep	selamat tidur	shee-lah-MAHT tee-DOR
happy travels	selamat jalan	shee-lah-MAHT jah-LAHN
sweet dreams	mimpi manis	MIHM-pee MAH-nees

Two girls greet a visitor to their home.

25

Indonesian students from Sulawesi clean their classroom before their teacher arrives.

Going to School

In Indonesia, kids get to school before their teachers. Some kids sweep the playground. Other kids water plants and trees in the school's garden.

Grades one through six are called Sekola Dasar, or SD. Students study math, reading, writing, history, government, religion, and social studies. In citizenship class, kids learn how to work together.

Hari Raya Saraswati

Balinese children and teachers celebrate Hari Raya Saraswati. Saraswati is honored as the goddess of learning. On Saraswati's day, no one reads books. No one plays instruments. And no one uses computers. Kids get the day off from school to honor Saraswati. They wear their nicest clothes. They pray together in the school yard. The smell of incense fills the air. Incense smells sweet when it is burned.

Children pray to Saraswati at a school on Bali.

27

Religion

Most Indonesians are Muslims. Muslims are people who practice Islam. In the big cities, you might hear the call to prayer. Sometimes the call comes over a crackly loudspeaker. People stop what they are doing. They kneel on the ground. Muslims face west when they pray. From Indonesia, that is the direction of Saudi Arabia. The religion of Islam came from there.

Children learn about Islam at a Muslim kindergarten on Sumatra.

Some Indonesians believe that all natural things—even plants, animals, and rocks—have a spirit. Many Indonesians hold this belief along with other religious beliefs, such as Hinduism.

Believers left these gifts of food and flowers for a spirit at a place of worship on Bali.

During Ramadan, adult Muslims eat only during the dark hours of the day.

Ramadan

Ramadan is the holiest time of year for Muslims. It takes place during the ninth month of the Islamic calendar. During Ramadan, adult Muslims fast. They do not eat or drink during the day.

Muslim families get up before dawn. They eat and drink as much as they like. At sunrise, Muslim villagers pray together. They do not eat for the rest of the day. Muslims pray again at sunset. After prayer, everyone can eat.

After Ramadan

The three days after Ramadan are called Eid al-Fitr. Families visit. They share special sweet treats and dates. People ask one another to forgive the wrongs they have done.

Boys in Jakarta carry torches in a parade marking the end of Ramadan and the beginning of Eid al-Fitr.

31

Wear a Sarong

Have you ever worn a sarong? A sarong is a piece of cloth that is 6 feet (2 m) long. People wrap it around their waists and tie it. In Indonesia, lots of people wear sarongs.

These girls are wearing sarongs. Both women and men wear sarongs in Indonesia.

To make a sarong, weavers use a thick cotton cloth called ikat. They use brown, deep red, and dark blue thread. They weave designs into the cloth. Pictures of birds, roses, and angels are popular.

This woman is weaving ikat cloth.

Shadow puppets tell an ancient Indonesian story.

Puppet Show

On the islands of Java and Bali, people gather to watch *wayang kulit*, or shadow puppets. The puppet shows happen late at night. A white screen hides the *dalang* (puppeteer) from the audience. The dalang moves the puppets to show a favorite folktale.

34

How Life Began

The Batak people tell this folktale to describe how life began.
One day, a god leaned against a tree. That made a branch fall into
the sea. From that branch came the fish and all ocean life. Another
branch fell to the ground. The branch created bugs and spiders.
A third branch broke into pieces. Each piece became a different
animal. An earthquake struck. And two birds laid eggs. The first
humans hatched from those eggs.

Priests of the Batak
people wrote down
some of their stories
in books made from
tree bark.

Music and Dance

Lots of bamboo trees grow in Indonesia. Musicians make instruments from bamboo. Schoolchildren of the Moluccas and Sulawesi play bamboo flutes. The children carry the flutes wherever they go.

A boy plays a bamboo instrument during a festival on Sulawesi.

36

Indonesian dances often tell stories. The movements of the dancers' heads, eyes, hands, and fingers are very meaningful. On Bali, dancers move to the music of drums, flutes, and gongs.

Balinese girls dance to the sound of drums and gongs.

Young Artists

Art is a big part of Indonesian life. People use bowls made by a potter. They wear handwoven sarongs. They sit on finely carved wood furniture.

A wood carver from Java finishes decorating a wooden table.

Kids in Indonesia learn to carve, paint, or weave as soon as they are old enough. Parents expect their children to be skilled crafters by about the age of twelve.

This girl is decorating wooden lily pads in her family's workshop in Bali.

39

Fast Food

Hungry? Look for people pushing little carts. They sell *bakso*, *satay*, or *gado-gado*. Bakso is a steaming bowl of soup. It is filled with vegetables, noodles, and little balls of meat. Satay is roasted chicken on a stick. Gado-gado is rice and vegetables. The dish is topped with a tasty peanut sauce. For dessert try *janjan*. Cooks make janjan with rice flour and raw sugar from the coconut palm.

A man sells bakso at a food cart in Bali.

Rambutan has a hairy, red peel. Inside it is a white, juicy, sweet fruit.

Tutti Frutti

Mangoes, bananas, pineapples, coconuts, and papayas grow in Indonesia. Try other fruits, such as the hairy red rambutan, the snake-skinned *salak*, or the honey-flavored *sawo*. All the fruit is really tasty.

41

Fly a Kite

What's that in the sky? Kites shaped like birds, bats, boxes, rocket ships, or butterflies float high. Kite festivals take place in March. Most Indonesian kids make their own kites. Kids join clubs to build really big ones. On the day of the festival, kids carry the huge kites to the beach. Ocean winds send the kites high in the air.

This family worked together on a giant butterfly kite.

Hundreds of people gather to watch a kite-flying festival on Bali.

THE FLAG OF INDONESIA

The Republic of Indonesia's flag has an upper red band and a lower white one. The flag was adopted on Independence Day, August 17, 1945. The red represents courage. The white represents the human spirit. Both are highly valued in Indonesia.

FAST FACTS

FULL COUNTRY NAME: Republic of Indonesia

AREA: 741,100 square miles (1,919,440 square kilometers). If you squeezed all the Indonesian islands together into one landmass, it would be about three times bigger than the state of Texas.

MAIN LANDFORMS: the mountain ranges Arfak, Barisan, Foja, Iran, Jayawijaya, Maoke, Muller, Schwaner, and Sudirman; the volcanoes Agung, Anak Krakatau, Batur, Bromo, Ciremai, Merapi, Semeru, and Tangkuban Prahu; and the forests

MAJOR RIVERS: Asahan, Barito, Brantas, Digul, Hari, Kapuas, Mamberamo, Musi, and Solo

ANIMALS AND THEIR HABITATS: orangutans, Asian elephants, birds of paradise, cockatoos, parrots, Sumatran rhinoceroes, Sumatran tigers, water buffalo (rain forests and forests); crocodiles, Komodo dragons (island of Komodo), wild boar; mackerel, mollusks, scad, sharks, tuna (ocean)

CAPITAL CITY: Jakarta

OFFICIAL LANGUAGE: Bahasa Indonesia

POPULATION: about 240,271,000

GLOSSARY

continent: any one of Earth's seven large areas of land. The continents are Africa, Antartica, Asia, Australia, Europe, North America, and South America.

earthquake: the shaking of the ground caused by the shifting of underground rock

erupt: to throw forth melted rock, ash, and smoke

ethnic group: a group of people with many things in common, such as language, religion, and customs

folktale: a story told by word of mouth from grandparent to parent to child. Many folktales explain where an ethnic group came from or how the world began.

incense: a material that gives off a sweet smell when burned

island: a piece of land that is smaller than a continent and is surrounded by water

plain: a broad, flat area of land that has few trees

plateau: a large area of high, level land

puppeteer: a person who stands behind a stage and makes a puppet move by hand

tsunami (soo-NAH-mee): a huge tidal wave caused by an underwater earthquake or volcano

volcano: an opening in Earth's surface through which hot, melted rock and gases shoot up. Volcano can also mean the hill or mountain of ash and rock that builds up around the opening.

TO LEARN MORE

BOOKS

Douglass, Susan L. *Ramadan.* Minneapolis: Millbrook Press, 2004. Learn about the month of Ramadan, during which Muslims around the world honor Allah.

Shepard, Aaron. *The Adventures of Mouse Deer: Indonesian and Malaysian Folktales.* Olympia, WA: Skyhook Press, 2008. This award-winning author retells the story of many animals that want to eat the mouse deer—who is small but brave and cunning—but first they have to catch him.

Waldmeier, Elisabeth. *Sadri Returns to Bali: A Tale of the Balinese Galungan Festival.* Hong Kong: Periplus, 2002. This story of Sadri is set during the exciting Galungan festival in Bali. The festival marks the victory of dharma (order) over adharma (disorder).

WEBSITES

Enchanted Learning
http://www.enchantedlearning.com/geography/abc/i.shtml
This site has pictures of Indonesia and its flag to label and color.

Indonesia
http://fotw.fivestarflags.com/id.html
Learn more about the history and meaning of the Indonesian flag at this site.

Indonesia
http://www.geographia.com/indonesia
See a detailed map and find out more about the geography and climate of Indonesia. This site also has links to information on specific areas of Indonesia with colorful photos of the Indonesian countryside.

INDEX

The photographs in this book are used with the permission of: © A & J Visage/Alamy, p. 4; © Ahmad Zamroni/AFP/Getty Images, p. 6; © Travel Ink/Gallo Images/Getty Images, p. 7; © Adek Berry/AFP/Getty Images, p. 8; © Tom Pfeiffer/VolcanoDiscovery/Photographer's Choice/Getty Images, p. 9; © Renaud Visage/The Image Bank/Getty Images, p. 10; © Pacific Stock/SuperStock, p. 11; © age fotostock/SuperStock, p. 12; © Cory Langley, pp. 13 (left), 23 (right), 41; © Pascal Goetgheluck/Photo Researchers, Inc., p. 13 (right); REUTERS/Beawiharta, p. 14; © WpN/Photoshot, p. 15; © Thomas Cockrem/Alamy, pp. 16, 18; © Thomas Pozzo Di Borgo/Dreamstime.com, p. 17; © Mitchell Kanashkevich/The Image Bank/Getty Images, p. 19; © Bay Ismoyo/AFP/Getty Images, p. 20; © Tom Cockrem/Lonely Planet Images, p. 21; © Robert Harding Picture Library/SuperStock, pp. 22, 33; © Jordan Siemens/Aurora/Getty Images, p. 23 (left); © Jefri Aries/ZUMA Press, p. 24; © Photononstop/SuperStock, pp. 25, 26; © Sonny Tumbelaka/AFP/Getty Images, p. 27; © @Painet Inc./Alamy, p. 28; © Roger Cracknell 01/classic/Alamy, p. 29; © Peter Ptschelinzew/Lonely Planet Images, p. 30; REUTERS/Supri, p. 31; © Cedric Lim/Asia Images/Getty Images, p. 32; © Mark Lewis/Alamy, p. 34; Book of Ritual Knowledge (Pustaha). 19th-early 20th century. Made in Indonesia, Sumatra, Toba Batak. Wood, bast, resin ink, fiber, H: 7 3/4 in. (19.7 cm). Gift of Fred and Rita Richman, 1988 (1988.143.133). Image copyright © The Metropolitan Museum of Art/Art Resource, NY, p. 35; © dbimages/Alamy, p. 36; © Jack Hollingsworth/Asia Images/Getty Images, p. 37; © craft images/Alamy, p. 38; © Imagestate Media Partners Limited - Impact Photos/Alamy, p. 39; © Michael Gebicki/Lonely Planet Images/Getty Images, p. 40; © Yadid Levy/Alamy, p. 42; © Jewel Samad/AFP/Getty Images, p. 43. Illustrations by © Bill Hauser/Independent Picture Service.

Cover: © Jeff Hunter/Photographer's Choice/Getty Images.